£2.49

C000110394

Wanderlust

www.wanderlust.co.uk

THE LITTLE BOOK OF

Wanderlust

Published by OH!
20 Mortimer Street
London W1T 3JW

Text © 2020 OH!
Design © 2020 OH!

Disclaimer:
All trademarks, quotations, company names, registered names,
products, characters, logos and catchphrases used or cited in this
book are the property of their respective owners. This book is a
publication of OH! An imprint of Welbeck Publishing Group
Limited and has not been licensed, approved, sponsored, or
endorsed by any person or entity. All rights reserved. No part of
this publication may be reproduced, stored in a retrieval system,
or transmitted in any form or by any means (including electronic,
mechanical, photocopying, recording, or otherwise) without prior
written permission from the publisher.

ISBN 978-1-80069-054-7

Compiled by: Hazel Plush
Editorial: Theresa Bebbington
Project manager: Russell Porter
Design: James Pople
Production: Rachel Burgess

A CIP catalogue record for this book is available from the British Library

Printed in Dubai

10 9 8 7 6 5 4 3 2 1

Images: freepik.com

THE LITTLE BOOK OF

Wanderlust

HAZEL PLUSH

Wanderlust

/ˈwɒn.də.lʌst/ [noun]

The wish to travel far away
and to many different places

Cambridge English Dictionary, 2020

"

Wanderlust is a yearning, an addiction, an itch that is always lying just under the surface of your skin. It may lie dormant or repressed for a while. But then there will be a whisper in your ear, a sound carried on the breeze, a whiff of tantalising spice – and the craving will return. Once you have wanderlust, you have it for life.

"

Lyn Hughes
Founder & Editor-in-chief, Wanderlust

CONTENTS

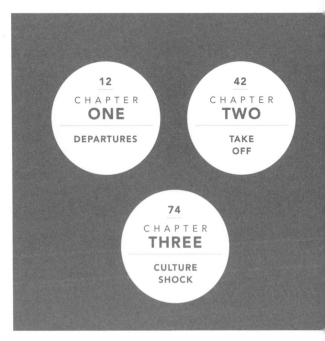

INTRODUCTION

Is it the lure of a road less travelled? The thrills and spills of a wild city break? Or simply the joy of a do-nothing-eat-everything week on the beach? Whatever sparks your wanderlust, one thing's for certain – you're in excellent company. Those who explore the world, you see, return home all the wiser – eyes open to new cultures, tastebuds tingling with new flavours, and ears attuned to new languages (even if it's just "*dos cervezas, por favor*").

From philosophers to poets, chefs to comedians, the world's greatest thinkers and doers are inspired by travel: it's their muse, their motivation, the fuel to their fire. But you know this already, of course – because it's your *raison d'etre*, too. You measure years in the number of holidays taken, harbour a secret enjoyment of in-flight food, and own more mini hotel toiletries than full-size ones. Your weakness? Suitcases. Your bedtime reading? Guidebooks. Every crisp, empty passport page is an irresistible challenge…

Some people might tell you to get it out of your system; others might say it's just a phase. But we know the truth: once you've got wanderlust, it's with you for life. And why would you want to stop globe-trotting, country-hopping, trip-plotting? This book, created by fellow travel-lovers, celebrates the joy of discovering pastures new. It's packed with wise words and fascinating facts, and is bursting with trivia titbits – indeed, it took all of our luggage-stuffing expertise just to cram everything in. We hope it inspires you to have even more adventures, both big and small – to cross borders, chase horizons and never stop travelling.

Where will your wanderlust take you?

CHAPTER ONE

DEPARTURES

WISE WORDS FROM THE WORLD'S
GREATEST TRAVELLERS

Nothing behind me, everything ahead of me, as is ever so on the road.

Jack Kerouac
On the Road, 1957

"

How big the world is, how big and how wonderful. It comes to me as ridiculously presumptuous that I should dare to carry my little personality halfway across it.

"

Gertrude Bell, in a letter to her cousin Horace Marshall, dated 18 June 1892.
Published in *The Letters of Gertrude Bell*, 1927

I haven't been everywhere,
but it's on my list.

Susan Sontag

"Unguided tour", *The New Yorker*, 1977

"

Take only memories,
leave only footprints.

Chief Si'ahl, leader of the Native American
Suquamish and Duwamish tribes.

Speech, 1850s (exact date unknown)

The real voyage of discovery consists not in seeking new landscapes, but in having new eyes.

Marcel Proust
La Prisonnière, 1923

> **"**
> If you think adventure is dangerous,
> try routine -- it's lethal.
> **"**

Paulo Coelho de Souza

Source: *Twitter* (@paulocoelho), November 2011

A journey of a thousand miles begins with a single step.

Lao Tzu

6th century BC (exact date unknown)

“

You would have to tie me to a tree to stop me travelling. As I get older and travel more, the world seems to open up to me, beckoning me and whispering in my ear saying 'Go'.

”

Joanna Lumley

Interview in *Wanderlust* magazine, September 2016

Travel changes you. As you move through this life and this world you change things slightly, you leave marks behind, however small. And in return, life – and travel – leaves marks on you.

Anthony Bourdain

Kitchen Confidential: Adventures in the Culinary Underbelly, 2000

If you look like your passport photo, in all probability you need the journey.

Earl Wilson

New York Post, date unknown

"

The truth is, you will never be ready. The only way to get ready for an adventure is to have one.

"

Lois Pryce

"Travel as a solo woman: 10 lessons for the intrepid", *The Telegraph*, 2015

66

Like all great travellers, I have seen more than I remember, and remember more than I have seen.

Benjamin Disraeli
Vivian Grey, 1826

99

"

'It's a dangerous business, Frodo, going out your door,' he used to say. 'You step into the road, and if you don't keep your feet, there is no knowing where you might be swept off to.'

"

Frodo, J.R.R. Tolkien's famous hobbit, recalls the wise words of his distant cousin Bilbo – as he sets off on the adventure of a lifetime. *The Fellowship of the Ring*, 1954

66

The world is a book, and those
who do not travel only read
one page.

99

Contrary to popular opinion, St Augustine
(born AD 354) may not be responsible
for this *bon mot*. Its original source is unknown.

There is much more light in the world than darkness… If you travel intelligently and give a damn about where you are, you can be a positive force for good. You can help protect and preserve iconic creatures and areas by your presence.

Simon Reeve

Interview in *The Independent*, May 2018

"

For always roaming with
a hungry heart
Much have I seen and known.

"

Alfred Tennyson

"Ulysses", 1842

DEPARTURES

Twenty years from now you will be more disappointed by the things you didn't do than by the ones you did. So throw off the bowlines. Sail away from the safe harbour. Catch the trade winds in your sails. Explore. Dream. Discover.

H. Jackson Brown Jr
P.S. I Love You, 1990

"

Christopher Robin was sitting outside his door, putting on his Big Boots.

As soon as he saw the Big Boots, Pooh knew that an Adventure was about to happen, and he brushed the honey off his nose with the back of his paw, and spruced himself up as well as he could, so as to look Ready for Anything.

"

A.A. Milne
Winnie-the-Pooh, 1926

"

A journey is a person in itself;
no two are alike. And all plans,
safeguards, policies and coercion
are fruitless. We find after years of
struggle that we do not take a
trip; a trip takes us.

"

John Steinbeck

Travels with Charley: In Search of America, 1962

66

The supreme moments of
travel are born of beauty
and strangeness.

99

Robert Byron

First Russia, Then Tibet, 1933

Life is either a daring adventure
or nothing.

Helen Keller
Let Us Have Faith, 1940

"

I have no reason to go, except that I have never been, and knowledge is better than ignorance. What better reason could there be for travelling?

"

Dame Freya Stark

A Winter in Arabia, 1940

"

The soul of the journey is liberty,
perfect liberty, to think, feel, do
just as one pleases.

"

William Hazlitt

Table Talk, 1821

"

For my part, I travel not to go anywhere, but to go. I travel for travel's sake. The great affair is to move; to feel the needs and hitches of our life more nearly; to come down off this feather-bed of civilisation, and find the globe granite underfoot.

"

Robert Louis Stevenson
Travels with a Donkey in the Cévennes, 1879

DEPARTURES

Travel is fatal to prejudice, bigotry, and narrow-mindedness, and many of our people need it sorely on these accounts. Broad, wholesome, charitable views of men and things cannot be acquired by vegetating in one little corner of the earth all one's lifetime.

Mark Twain
The Innocents Abroad, 1869

"

To move, to breathe, to fly, to float,
To gain all while you give,
To roam the roads of lands remote,
To travel is to live.

"

Hans Christian Andersen

The Fairy Tale of My Life: An Autobiography, 1847

66

Because in the end, you won't remember the time you spent working in the office or mowing your lawn. Climb that goddamn mountain.

99

Jack Kerouac often gets the credit for this wise nugget – but apparently the great Beat Generation author never actually said it himself. It was published in *Esquire* magazine's "The 80 Best Books Every Man Should Read", in a *description* of Kerouac's 1958 novel *The Dharma Bums*.

Esquire, 2010

66

A rolling stone gathers no moss.

Publilius Syrus

The Moral Sayings of Publius Syrus:
A Roman Slave (published 1st century BC;
exact date unknown)

99

CHAPTER TWO

TAKE OFF

TRAINS, PLANES, RICKSHAWS,
UNICYCLES... LIFE'S ALWAYS BETTER
WHEN YOU'RE ON THE MOVE

90

The average length, in seconds, of the world's shortest commercial flight. It connects the Scottish islands of Westray and Papa Westray: a distance of just 2.7km (1.6 miles) – that's shorter than either of Heathrow's runways.

Source: "The world's shortest flight may soon be its greenest, too", *The Economist*, August 2019

"

Rumack: Can you fly this plane
   and land it?
Striker: Surely you can't be serious?
Rumack: I am serious. And don't
   call me Shirley.

"

Facing his fear of flying, Ted Striker
(Robert Hays) takes control in *Airplane!* (1980)
– and hands Dr Rumack (Leslie Nielsen) one
of the best-loved lines in movie history

TAKE OFF

We'd have more luck playing pick-up sticks with our butt-cheeks than we will getting a flight out of here before daybreak.

99

Neal Page (Steve Martin) and Del Griffith (John Candy) discover they're stuck in Wichita – just one of their travel trials in *Planes, Trains and Automobiles* (1987).

10

The number of chandeliers lighting up the main concourse of New York's famous Grand Central Terminal station. Each one of the century-old lamps is adorned with gold detailing, and holds 110 bulbs (compact fluorescent ones, naturally – in line with the city's environmental goals).

Source: "At Grand Central, a fluorescent twist to a light-bulb joke", *The New York Times*, April 2009

-51

The average temperature, in degrees Celsius, outside your plane window while cruising at 35,000ft (10,670m). Look closely, and you might spot a tiny hole at the bottom of the window: this is a 'bleed hole', designed to help balance the air pressure and prevent fogging or frosting on the pane.

Sources: *livescience.com*, 2012; *baatraining.com*, 2018

66

The journey is the reward.

99

Chinese proverb (date unknown)

Few places are more conducive to internal conversations than a moving plane, ship or train. There is an almost quaint correlation between what is in front of our eyes and the thoughts we are able to have in our heads: large thoughts at times requiring large views, new thoughts new places.

Introspective reflections which are liable to stall are helped along by the flow of the landscape. The mind may be reluctant to think properly when thinking is all it is supposed to do.

99

Alain de Botton

The Art of Travel, 2002

TAKE OFF

Have you flown far?

Dan McCallon, an Irish farmhand, makes small talk with **Amelia Earhart** after he sees her landing in a pasture in Northern Ireland, on the morning of 20 May 1932. "From America," replied the pioneering aviator. Earhart had just become the first woman to fly solo nonstop across the Atlantic, having taken off from Newfoundland 14 hours, 56 minutes ago.

Life magazine, 2002

Q: Which mode of transport gets its name from the 'spluttering' sound that its engine makes?

Source: "12 facts that nobody told you about tuk tuks", atuktuk. com, January 2020

A: Tuk tuk. These little motorised taxis, prevalent in Asia, are also known as auto rickshaws.

1802

The year that the first design for the Channel Tunnel was drawn up by French engineer Albert Mathieu. He proposed to light the tunnel with oil lamps and create a halfway point for changing horses.

Sources: *The Telegraph*, 2019; *eurotunnel.com*

"

Do you know you have never lived until you have flown?

"

Bessie Coleman, the first woman of African-American or Native-American descent to hold a pilot's licence.

Chicago Defender, 1921

We climb into the bus and sit down. At this point there is a risk of culture clash, of collision and conflict. It will undoubtedly occur if the passenger is a foreigner who doesn't know Africa. Someone like that will start looking around, squirming, inquiring, 'When will the bus leave?'

'What do you mean, *when*?'
the astonished driver will reply.
'It will leave when we find enough
people to fill it up.'

Ryszard Kapuściński on the nuances
of Ghanaian bus travel.
The Shadow of the Sun, 1998

TAKE OFF

"

Label your luggage legibly and boldly. The name of the place should be in larger letters than the name of the person; however much this may offend our self-esteem, it must be borne in mind that, in the hurry and bustle of departure, the destination is what is first required to be known – the owner being a secondary consideration.

"

Anonymous
The Railway Traveller's Handy Book, 1862

18,000

The number of passengers, per hour, that the world's highest cable car can carry. Mi Teleferico – in La Paz, Bolivia – is one of the world's most unusual commutes, whisking workers between the city centre and El Alto, a district in the mountains. It is 11km (over 6.8 miles) long, and cost US$234 million (£188.5 million) to build.

Source: "10 of the world's best cable car rides", *cnn.com*, April 2017

2,172

The cruising speed of Concorde, in kilometres per hour: that's more than twice the speed of sound. During flight, the 62m (203-ft)-long airframe stretched by up to 25.4cm (12in), thanks to the heat generated by its supersonic flight.

Source: *British Airways*

66

Airplane travel is nature's way
of making you look like your
passport photo.

99

Al Gore

The World According to Gore, 2007

TAKE OFF

When dealing with complex transportation issues, the best thing to do is pull up with a cold beer and let somebody else figure it out.

Anthony Bourdain gives a masterclass in logistics, in season one of his CNN travelogue "Parts Unknown" (2013)

Q: By passenger numbers, which is the busiest airport in the world?

A: Hartsfield-Jackson Atlanta International Airport, in Georgia, USA. A total of 110,531,300 passengers used the airport in 2019.

Source: internationalairportreview.com, 2020

70,000

The number of bottles of champagne that were consumed on the *QE2* ocean liner every year, before her retirement in 2008.

Source: "50 remarkable facts about the QE2", *The Telegraph*, September 2017

"

Tea at the refreshment rooms
of railway stations and on board
steamboats is often a mere
parody on the real article –
a fearful decoction.

"

Lillias Campbell Davidson

Hints to Lady Travellers, 1889

66

I never travel without my diary. One should always have something sensational to read in the train.

99

Gwendolen Fairfax shares her top travel tip in Oscar Wilde's *The Importance of Being Earnest* (1895)

959 million

The cost, in pounds sterling (US$1.2 billion), to build *Symphony of the Seas* – the world's biggest cruise ship. It can carry up to 5,518 passengers, and employs 2,200 crew members (not including the cocktail-making robots in its Bionic Bar).

Source: "Everything you need to know about the world's largest cruise ship", *The Telegraph*, March 2018

320

The top speed, in km/hour
(199mph), of Japan's Shinkansen
'bullet' trains – the fastest trains
on the planet. They're efficient,
too: the entire fleet has an average
delay time of just 60 seconds.
The service has nine lines, the
first of which opened in 1964.

Sources: *jrailpass.com*; *traveller.com.au*;
Encyclopædia Britannica

Q: 'Peggo', 'Opal' and 'Beep' are the local brand names of which travel essential?

A: Prepaid public transport cards – in Winnipeg, Canada; New South Wales, Australia; and Manila, Philippines respectively.

Source: "List of smart cards", wikpedia.org, 2020

It can hardly be a coincidence that no language on Earth has ever produced the phrase, 'as pretty as an airport'. Airports are ugly. Some are very ugly. Some attain a degree of ugliness that can only be the result of a special effort.

Douglas Adams

The Long Dark Tea-Time of the Soul, 1988

100

The number of hairpin bends on a 30km (18.6 mile) stretch of the 'Three Level Zigzag Road' – which winds its way through the lower Himalayas in Sikkim, India. Its pinnacle is the Thambi viewpoint, which looks out over the mountains from an altitude of almost 3,500m (11,480ft). White knuckles guaranteed.

Source: "Three Level Zigzag Road", *dangerousroads.org*

TAKE OFF

Q: Germany's Coradia iLint train is a world-leading example of eco-friendly transport – but what powers it?

Sources: "Next stop, hydrogen-powered trains", BBC Future Planet, February 2020; alstom.com

A: Hydrogen. Its only exhaust is steam and condensed water.

I look for the unfamiliar. I love going to places where I feel like an explorer of sorts – and that doesn't mean that you have to go to the other end of the world.

Kate Humble
Interview in *Wanderlust* magazine, 2014

CHAPTER THREE

CULTURE SHOCK

THE WORLD IS FULL OF SURPRISES

Travel is good for your brain!
With every new experience or
challenge, the brain creates new
connections – which ultimately
boost your cognitive health.
So book that city tour, try a new
skill or learn some local lingo
– your grey matter will thank you.

Source: "Travel as a health regimen",
Chicago Tribune, January 2014

> 66
>
> One's destination is never a place, but a new way of looking at things.
>
> 99

Henry Miller

Big Sur and the Oranges of Hieronymus Bosch, 1957

Q: 'Prairie oysters' are a delicacy in Canada, but what exactly are they?

A: Bulls' testicles. They're served sautéed, fried, stuffed – however you like.

Between the woven leaves of some Vietnamese conical hats known as *non la*, lie hidden poems and drawings. They are invisible, unless the hat is held up to the light.

Source: "Non la", *vietnamonline.com*

The world's biggest baguette consumer is Algeria, not France. The North African nation consumes 49 million baguettes every day.

Source: "Algeria's love affair with baguettes", *world-grain.com*, January 2016

"

Every traveller has two or three
or even a hundred of them:
moments on a journey when
you taste something and you're
forever changed.

"

James Oseland

A Fork in the Road, 2013

Q: In Scotland, haggis is traditionally served with 'neeps and tatties' – but what exactly are they?

A: Turnips/swedes and potatoes

Barcelona's Sagrada Família cathedral, designed by Antoni Gaudí, has been under construction for the last 138 years. It's expected to be completed in 2026.

The Arabic language has hundreds of words for 'camel'. For example, *al-jafool* means 'a camel that's frightened by anything'.

Source: "A few surprising facts about the Arabic language", *britishcouncil.org*, December 2015

"

You have to find out for yourself. Take the leap – go as far as you can. Try staying out of touch. Become a stranger in a strange land. Learn the language. Listen to what people are saying.

"

Paul Theroux

Fresh-air Fiend: Travel Writings, 2011

CULTURE SHOCK

If you reject the food, ignore the customs, fear the religion and avoid the people, you might better stay home.

James A. Michener
Holiday magazine, March 1956

Japan has a museum devoted to Pot Noodles. There's also The Big Mac Museum (in Pennsylvania, USA) and The Museum of Tap Water (in Beijing, China).

Vatican City has the world's highest wine consumption per capita. The average citizen drinks 54.26 litres (9.5 pints) per year.

Source: *The Wine Institute*, 2013

Q: Which Caribbean country almost ran out of beer in 2016?

Caterpillars, perhaps. Big moth caterpillars in New Guinea that you put on a fire to burn off the hairs. They come out like Twiglets. **"**

Sir David Attenborough on being asked, "What is the most exotic thing you have ever eaten?"

"An interview with David Attenborough", *National Geographic magazine*, December 2008

In the wilds of Argentinian Patagonia, there is a tiny Welsh-speaking community: Y Wladfa. It is populated by descendents of Welsh immigrants who arrived in the 1800s. The local cafés serve a mean *bara brith* (Welsh fruit bread).

Spain's national anthem
has no lyrics.

Alex Marshall

*Republic or Death! Travels in
Search of National Anthems, 2015*

Q: Poutine, a Canadian dish, consists of chips topped with... ?

A: Cheese curds and gravy

CULTURE SHOCK

66

For day wear, Palm Beach shirts or light suits are general… revolvers are unnecessary.

99

Author unknown

The South American Handbook, 1947

The Panama hat originated, in fact, in Ecuador.

Source: "Panama hat origin and history", *genuinepanamahats.co.uk*, March 2019

Vending machines aren't just for snacks: Singapore has one that sells books, while some in Taiwan and Malaysia dispense Hello Kitty toys, socks and shampoo.

Source: "10 of the world's weirdest vending machines", *Rough Guides*, April 2020

Meanwhile, in Dubai, you can buy gold from a vending machine: the prices fluctuate in real-time, according to the market value.

Source: "UAE unveils world's first gold bar vending machine", *arabianbusiness.com*, 2010

Q: Which country is home to the world's biggest wine cellar?

A: Moldova. The Mileștii Mici cellar is approximately 150 miles (240km) long.

"

Travel broadens the mind, but also the hips unfortunately (because who can resist sampling new cuisine?)

"

Kathy Lette

Quoted in *The Little Blue Book of Travel Wisdom*, 2014

66

Travelling is the ruin of all happiness! There's no looking at a building here after seeing Italy.

99

Fanny Burney
Cecilia, 1782

66

To travel is to discover that everyone is wrong about other countries.

99

Aldous Huxley

Along the Road: Notes and Essays of a Tourist, 1989

Q: Peru grows 3,800 different varieties of which vegetable?

A: Potatoes. They were first cultivated on the shores of Lake Titicaca 10,000 years ago. (And yes, botanically speaking, a potato is definitely a vegetable.)

Source: "The 3800 different types of potatoes in Peru", *limaeasy.com*

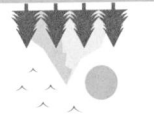

CHAPTER FOUR

BUCKET LIST

BIG CITIES, BREATHTAKING BEACHES,
ANCIENT TREASURES... WHERE ARE
YOU DREAMING OF?

BUCKET LIST

Antarctica is the 'driest' continent on Earth, despite its abundance of ice and snow. With an average precipitation of 50mm (2in) per year, the Antarctic Ice Sheet is technically the largest desert in the world – despite also being the largest single body of fresh water (mostly in the form of ice).

Source: *Guinness World Records*

Q: Which Caribbean island has 365 beaches – one for every day of the year?

226

The number of Michelin stars awarded to Tokyo's restaurants in 2019. It is the world's most Michelin-decorated city.

Source: *Guinness World Records*

Jet lag feels worse if you travel
from west to east.

Source: "Jet lag disorder", *Mayo Clinic*, 2018

BUCKET LIST

Russia is larger than Pluto.
By surface area, the country
measures 17.1 million km²
(6.6 million sq miles), while the
planet measures 16.7 million km²
(6.4 million sq miles). Russia is
also almost twice as large as
Canada, the second largest
country on Earth.

By contrast, Vatican City is the smallest country in the world, measuring 0.44km² (0.17 sq miles). That's around a third of the size of Hyde Park.

Q: Until 1904, 'Longacre Square' was the name of which famous attraction?

A: Times Square, New York City

160

The number of storeys in the Burj Khalifa, Dubai. At 828m (2,716ft) high, it is the tallest building in the world.

Source: *burjkhalifa.ae*

90

The percentage of a sloth's life that it spends upside down. You'll find them hanging out in Central America and South America, happily sleeping, eating, mating and even giving birth upside down.

Sources: *World Animal Protection*, 2017; *Smithsonian National Zoological Park*, 2019

The Micronesian island of Yap uses rocks as a currency: their value is based on their size and history. For everyday purchases, US dollars are used – but the stones (known as *rai*) are vital for ceremonial transactions.

Source: "The tiny island with human-sized money", *BBC Travel*, May 2018

BUCKET LIST

Your holiday destination says more about you than you might realise. Introverts tend to prefer trips into the mountains, while extroverts are happiest at the seaside.

Source: *Journal of Research in Personality*, University of Virginia, 2015

270,000

The number of islands in Sweden – though just 984 are inhabited. It has more islands than any other country in the world, making it a glorious spot for summer cruise holidays.

Sources: *Statistics Sweden*, 2014; "The countries with the most islands (and the idyllic ones you must visit)", *The Telegraph*, 2018

BUCKET LIST

Many travellers dream of seeing the Northern Lights – but the Southern Lights, or aurora australis, are just as spectacular. They blaze red, orange, pink and green across the Southern Hemisphere's skies.

Source: "Where and when to see the Southern Lights", *Wanderlust* magazine, September 2019

Q: The Northern Lights are visible from the village of Å, but which country is it in?

20

The number of years that the Eiffel Tower was supposed to be erected for – yet it's still standing 131 years after it was constructed.

Source: *toureiffel.paris*

Q: Which London hotel was the first in the world to have en-suite bathrooms for every bedroom?

A: The Savoy

BUCKET LIST

Sudan has more ancient pyramids than Egypt – roughly twice as many, in fact.

Source: "The surprising country with more pyramids than Egypt", *The Telegraph*, September 2019

1,000

The estimated number of rabbits running wild on Ōkunoshima Island, Japan. They far outnumber the human population, and nobody is quite sure how they got there.

Source: "This island is overrun with rabbits", *National Geographic* magazine, December 2017

Q: What was the original purpose of the Leaning Tower of Pisa?

A: Bell tower

Table Mountain, in South Africa, is often covered in a thin white cloud – known as the 'table cloth'.

Source: *tablemountainnationalpark.org*

1

The percentage of The Maldives that lies above the ocean. The rest of the country is below sea level – and offers some of the best scuba diving in the world.

Q: What is the capital city of Australia?

A: Canberra

Q: Which country has the longest official name in the world?

A: The United Kingdom of Great Britain and Northern Ireland

Bhutan is the world's only carbon-negative country. Over 60 per cent of its landmass is covered in forest, and it has won records for planting the most trees per hour.

Source: "Visit the world's only carbon-negative country", *National Geographic* magazine, 2017

At Disneyland Park, California, the character of Mickey Mouse is often played by a woman: you have to be shorter than 5ft 2in (157.5cm) to fit in the costume.

Source: "The secrets of the Happiest Place On Earth – 17 things I learnt working at Disney World", *The Telegraph*, July 2019

820

The number of languages spoken in Papua New Guinea, making it the country with the highest linguistic diversity.

Source: "What languages are spoken in Papua New Guinea?", *worldatlas.com*

Q: Which city starred as 'King's Landing', in the HBO drama *Game of Thrones*?

A: Dubrovnik, Croatia

When explorer Hiram Bingham 'found' Machu Picchu in 1911, he was actually looking for the ancient city of Vilcabamba. Of course, Machu Picchu had never really been 'lost': local people knew exactly where it was. When Bingham arrived, three families of farmers were living among the fabled mountaintop ruins.

Sources: *Encyclopaedia Britannica*, 2020; "Discover 10 secrets of Machu Picchu", *National Geographic* magazine, 2018

CHAPTER FIVE

TRAILBLAZERS

FOR SOME, A BEACH HOLIDAY
IS NEVER ENOUGH

I had to choose between selling margarine and adventure.
I chose adventure.

Sir Chris Bonington, the celebrated mountaineer, on turning down a job with Unilever in his youth – and heading to South America instead.

Quoted in *Explorers' Sketchbooks*, 2016

"

I focus on the doorway and the inky black beyond. One step is all you have to do. Take a leap of faith. **"**

Explorer **Bonita Norris** digs deep on her quest to climb Mount Everest.

The Girl Who Climbed Everest, 2017

It seemed difficult at first to grasp that we'd got there… But as the fact of our success thrust itself more clearly into my mind, I felt a quiet glow of satisfaction spread through my body. I turned and looked at Tenzing. Even beneath his oxygen mask and the icicles hanging from his hair, I could see his infectious grin of sheer delight. I held out my hand, and in silence we shook in good Anglo-Saxon fashion. But this was not enough for Tenzing, and impulsively he threw his arm around my shoulders and we thumped each other on the back in mutual congratulations. "

Sir Edmund Hillary recounts summiting Mount Everest with Sherpa Tenzing Norgay, on 29 May 1953. They were the first ever climbers confirmed to have reached the top.

"Arrival at the summit" (1953), published in *The Oxford Book of Exploration*, 1993

On his 1910 expedition to the South Pole, Norwegian explorer Roald Amundsen fitted out his ship – the *Fram* – with 3,000 books, a gramophone, a piano and some mandolins. He knew how demoralising boredom could get for crews, and his plan worked: the team was the first to reach the South Pole, in December 1911.

Source: *Expeditions Unpacked: What the Great Explorers Took into the Unknown*, 2019

"

I honestly didn't realise what a big deal it was.

"

Jan Morris, on reporting the story of Hillary and Tenzing's successful summit of Everest. She wrote the article in a tent in the Himalayas, by the light of a hurricane lamp.

Quoted in *Explorers' Sketchbooks*, 2016

"

It's very funny – around here the idea of a woman travelling alone is so completely outside the experience and beyond the imagination of everyone that it's universally assumed I'm a man. This convenient illusion is fostered by the very short haircut I deliberately got in Tehran…

"

Dervla Murphy blends in while cycling around Iran.
Full Tilt: Ireland to India with a Bicycle, 1965

In 2018, Ed Pratt became the first person to unicycle around the world. The Somerset-born adventurer took three years to complete the journey of 33,000km, (20,500 miles) raising over £300,000 (US$391,000) for charity.

Source: "Unicyclist Ed Pratt completes round-the-world trip", *BBC News*, July 2018

Back in 1955, I went to Indonesia specifically to try and find birds of paradise, but we weren't even let in. We turned up in Jakarta with a camera, didn't speak a word of Malay and didn't have a letter of introduction from anybody. It was ridiculous. When we said we wanted to go to Aru Island they said no. At the time they [the government] were trying to claim the island from Holland

and they thought we were spies. So we hastily thought of something else and went off to film Komodo dragons – but we didn't get that either. It was hopelessly amateur and cack-handed but quite good fun.

Sir David Attenborough recalls the haphazard ways of his early television-presenting career.

"An interview with David Attenborough", *National Geographic* magazine, December 2008

Lake Disappointment, in Western Australia, was so-named in 1897 by the explorer Frank Hann because he had expected to find a large freshwater lake – yet this one was largely dry.

Source: J.S. Beard, *Journal of the Royal Society of Western Australia*, 2005

....

Australia is also home to a Mount
Disappointment, in Victoria, whose
summit views failed to impress
British explorers Hamilton Hume
and William Hovell when they
climbed it in 1824.

Source: *Journey of Discovery to Port Phillip*, 1837

....

We crawled out of our igloos and found a dense mist hanging over everything. Only at intervals, when the sun's rays managed to penetrate the mist, could we catch even a glimpse of the sky.

Matthew Henson, disputably the first explorer to reach the North Pole, writes in his diary on 6 April 1909.

Quoted in *The Adventure Gap*, 2014

66

Distance changes utterly when you take the world on foot. A mile becomes a long way, two miles literally considerable, ten miles whopping, 50 miles at the very limits of conception. The world, you realise, is enormous in a way that only you and a small community of fellow hikers know. Planetary scale is your little secret.

99

Bill Bryson contemplates the vast distance of the Appalachian Trail (all 2,190 miles/3,525km of it).
A Walk in the Woods, 1997

[Since leaving England] my mind has been in a perfect hurricane of delight and astonishment.

Sir Charles Darwin writes home from Botafogo Bay, Brazil, in May 1832.

Published in *The Correspondence of Charles Darwin, Volume 1*, 1985

66

Every day is a daring adventure, a trip into the joyful pursuit of our full human potential. Along this path we try, and often fail. But we persevere. We persist. Only then do we succeed.

99

James Edward Mills, on the first all-African-American summit attempt on Denali – the highest point in North America.

"About the Joy Trip project", *joytripproject.com*

In her quest to beat the fictional Phileas Fogg's 80-day global circumnavigation, American journalist Nellie Bly whizzed around the world by train, steamship, rickshaw, horse and donkey – arriving back in New Jersey on 5 January 1890, just 72 days after she departed. Her editor at the *New York World* newspaper had initially doubted her capabilities: 'No one but a man can do this,' he told her. 'Very well,' she replied, 'Start the man, and I'll start the same day for some other newspaper and beat him.'

Source: "Nellie Bly's record-breaking trip around the world was, to her surprise, a race", *Smithsonian* magazine, January 2016

The sand is maddening. It fills your hair, your eyes, your water bottles; silts up your colour box; dries into your skies; and reduces your Chinese white to a gritty paste the colour of salad dressing. As for the flies, they have a morbid appetite for watercolours.

Amelia Edwards, author, painter and renowned Egyptologist – on the trials of working in the desert in the 1800s.
A Thousand Miles Up the Nile, 1877

A 104-year-old biscuit, which was originally carried by polar explorer Ernest Shackleton on a voyage to Antarctica, sold for US$2,000 (£1,627) at Christie's auction house in 2011. Made by British company Huntley and Palmers, the biscuit was left over from the thousands that sustained Shackleton and his team on the 1907–1909 *Nimrod* expedition.

Source: "Explorer Ernest Shackleton's biscuit sells for $2,000", *Business Insider*, September 2011

Since it was founded 130 years ago, the National Geographic Society has awarded more than 13,000 grants and supported the work of more than 3,000 explorers in the field.

Source: "Here's what it really means to become a National Geographic explorer", *National Geographic* magazine, June 2018

"

Sometimes a journey arises out of hope and instinct, the heady conviction, as your finger travels along the map: Yes, here and here… and here. These are the nerve ends of the world.

"

Colin Thubron tries to put his finger on what constitutes an adventure.
Shadow of the Silk Road, 2006

There was one severe blizzard during our crossing of the Antarctic continent, and we had a few hours waiting for the worst storm to subside. My fellow explorer, Mike Stroud, drew a chessboard on the lid of the cooking pot. Because he was doing detailed scientific tasks during the expedition, he had pee bottles. Mine were red and his blue. Some of them full, some not. We played chess with pee bottles, basically. He taught me how to play and then consistently won. "

Sir Ranulph Fiennes, on finding entertainment in the unlikeliest of places.

"Ranulph Fiennes: You ask the questions", *The Independent*, 2003

The two important things that I did learn were that you are as powerful and strong as you allow yourself to be, and that the most difficult part of any endeavour is taking the first step, making the first decision.

Robyn Davidson, on trekking across 1,700 miles (2,735km) of the Australian outback, with only four camels and a dog for company.

Tracks, 1980

About 500 years before Christopher Columbus was even born, legend has it that Leif Eriksson – a Viking explorer – became the first European to 'discover' North America. After crossing the Atlantic, his expedition encountered a rocky, barren land in present-day Canada: Eriksson called it 'Helluland', meaning 'Land of Flat Rocks'.

Source: "The Viking explorer who beat Columbus to America", *History.com*, October 2013

Exploring is part of being human; people have always wanted to know what lies beyond the next mountain or across a faraway river. Partly it is just our natural curiosity: what is a place like? What would it be like to live there?

Alan Bean, US Navy test pilot and NASA astronaut, on the enduring appeal of travel – both earthly and cosmic.

Quoted in *Explorers' Sketchbooks*, 2016

66

Not all those who wander
are lost.

99

Bilbo Baggins, the trailblazing hobbit, describes
Aragorn in "The Riddle of Strider".
The Fellowship of the Ring, 1954

CHAPTER SIX

HOMEWARD BOUND

PUT THE KETTLE ON AND
STASH THE SUITCASES. IT'S TIME
FOR SOME SERIOUS LAUNDRY

There's no such thing as a bad trip, just good travel stories to tell back home.

Patricia Schultz
1,000 Places to See Before You Die, 2003

66

No one realises how beautiful
it is to travel until he comes home
and rests his head on his old,
familiar pillow.

99

Lin Yutang

With Love And Irony, 1940

Travel makes one modest, you
see what a tiny place you occupy
in the world.

Gustave Flaubert
19th century (exact date unknown)

I met a lot of people in Europe.
I even encountered myself.

James Baldwin

(date unknown)

The post-holiday blues are real, with 57 per cent of Britons saying they feel 'deflated' after arriving home from a trip – so how to beat it? Experts recommend unpacking as soon as possible and giving yourself a few days before heading back to work.

Source: "How to beat post-holiday blues", *The Mirror*, September 2017

Homesickness is real, too. If you're worried about pining for home, try taking a few familiar things with you: some teabags, comfy slippers or a favourite novel perhaps?

Travel is glamorous only
in retrospect.

Paul Theroux
Washington Post, 1979

66

Often I feel I go to some distant region of the world to be reminded of who I really am.

99

Michael Crichton

Travels, 1988

HOMEWARD BOUND

"

Why do you go away? So that you can come back. So that you can see the place you came from with new eyes and extra colours. And the people there see you differently, too. Coming back to where you started is not the same as never leaving.

"

Sir Terry Pratchett
A Hat Full of Sky, 2004

"

Coming back to your native land after an absence of many years is a surprisingly unsettling business, a little like waking from a long coma.

"

Bill Bryson

I'm a Stranger Here Myself, 1998

The further you go… the harder it is to return. The world has many edges and it's easy to fall off.

Anderson Cooper

Dispatches From The Edge: A Memoir of War, Disasters, and Survival, 2006

66

There is nothing like returning to a place that remains unchanged to find the ways in which you yourself have altered.

99

Nelson Mandela

A Long Walk to Freedom, 1994

When his owners moved house, Howie – a Persian cat – wandered 1,000 miles (1,600km) through the Australian outback to get home. The journey took him 12 months.

Source: "Scientists don't quite know how this cat managed its trek home", *Smithsonian* magazine, January 2013

The end of all our exploring
Will be to arrive where we started
And know the place for the first time.

T.S. Eliot
"Little Gidding", 1942

HOMEWARD BOUND

Travel brings power and love back into your life.

Jalaluddin Rumi

(date unknown)

"

You know now that such a place exists and that you can get back to it someday if you want to, and it is satisfying to have that certainty.

Paul Bowles
Travels: Collected Writings, 1950–93, 2010

HOMEWARD BOUND

Paradise was always over there, a day's sail away. But it's a funny thing, escapism. You can go far and wide and you can keep moving on and on through places and years, but you never escape your own life. I, finally, knew where my life belonged. Home.

J. Maarten Troost

Getting Stoned with Savages: A Trip Through the Islands of Fiji and Vanuatu, 2006

To nest, female sea turtles return to the very beach where they were born – sometimes travelling thousands of miles to get there. Males, however, almost never return to land after hatching.

Source: *conserveturtles.org*

Travel, in the younger sort, is a part of education; in the elder, a part of experience.

Sir Francis Bacon

Essays or Counsels, Civil and Moral, 1595

❝

The whole object of travel is not to set foot on foreign land; it is at last to set foot on one's own country as a foreign land.

❞

G.K. Chesterton

Tremendous Trifles, 1909

Arrived home… without your suitcases? Over 20 million bags go missing at airports every year. Those that aren't claimed are often auctioned off at 'lost luggage' sales: you can bid on sealed suitcases with no knowledge of what's inside – and hopefully snap up a bargain or two.

Sources: "Why do airlines still mislay 25 million bags a year?", *BBC News*, June 2019; "Lost luggage auctions", *Money Saving Expert*, April 2019

66

Travelling – it leaves you speechless, then turns you into a storyteller.

99

Ibn Battuta

A Masterpiece to Those Who Contemplate the Wonders of Cities and the Marvels of Travelling, 1360s (exact date unknown)

Travel far enough, you
meet yourself.

David Mitchell
Cloud Atlas, 2004

If your holiday feels like it's over too soon, blame your brain. Scientists say that discovering new places can slow down your perception of time – but when things become familiar, the hours seem to speed up. That's why your return journey often feels shorter than the outward one.

Source: "The science of why time DOES seem to fly on the way home from holiday", *Daily Mail*, July 2015

HOMEWARD BOUND

It suddenly struck me that that tiny pea, pretty and blue, was the Earth. I put up my thumb and shut one eye, and my thumb blotted out the planet Earth. I didn't feel like a giant. I felt very, very small.

Neil Armstrong

Date unknown. Quoted in "Right here, right now", *earthobservatory.nasa.gov*, October 2017

66

Don't ask yourself what the world needs. Ask yourself what makes you come alive and then go do that. Because what the world needs is people who have come alive.

99

Howard Thurman

Quoted in *Violence Unveiled*, 1996

The world is a strange and wonderful place of infinite variety. Be bold and brave and take a punt on a place that you know nothing about.

Alastair Humphreys

Microadventures: Local Discoveries for Great Escapes, 2014

www.wanderlust.co.uk